INTO THE UNKNOWN

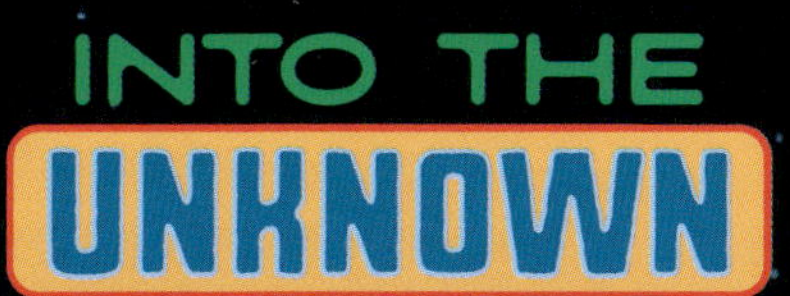

DO ALIENS VISIT EARTH?

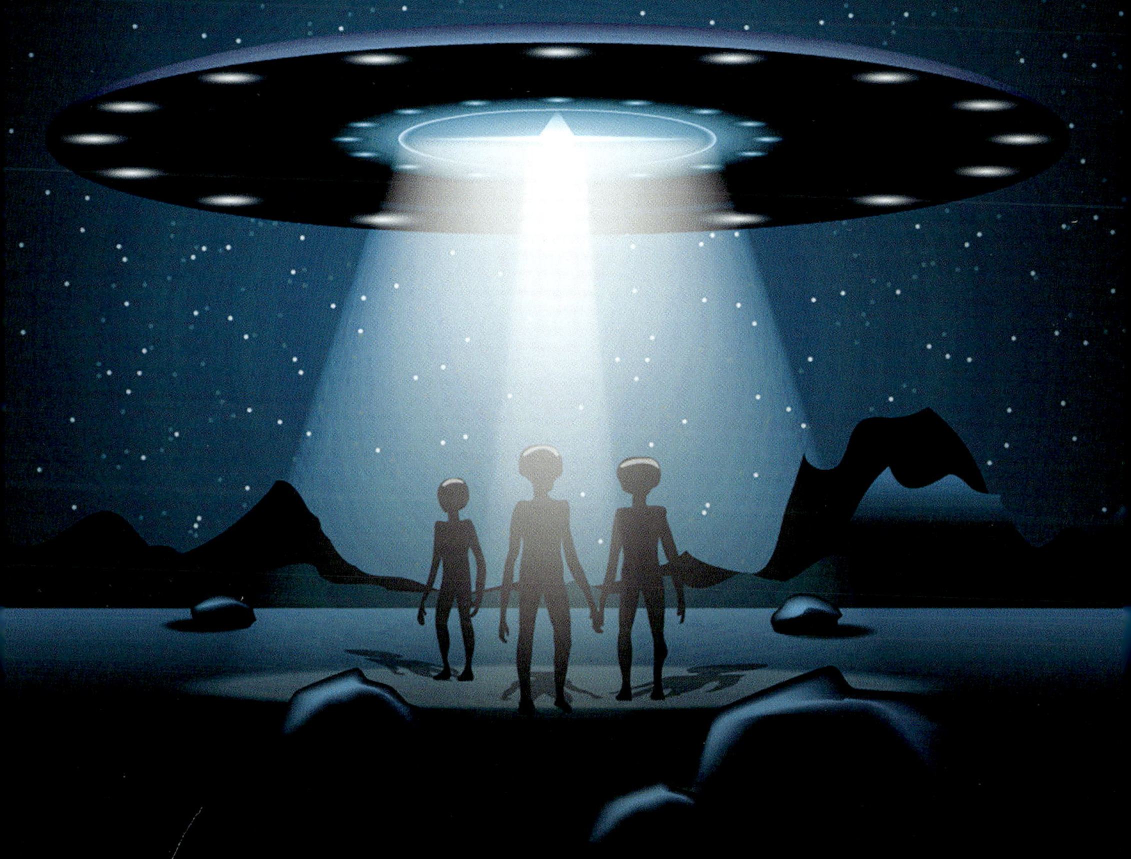

Kevin Cunningham

Mitchell Lane PUBLISHERS

Mitchell Lane
PUBLISHERS

mitchelllanepub.com

2001 SW 31st Avenue
Hallandale, FL 33009

First Edition, 2026.
Author: Kevin Cunningham
Designer: Ed Morgan
Editor: Morgan Brody

Series: Into the Unknown
Title: Do Aliens Visit Earth?

Library bound ISBN: 979-8-89260-735-3
eBook ISBN: 979-8-89260-744-5

Photo credits: cover, 13, 15, 23, 25 freepik.com; p. 5, 7, 27 Alamy; p. 9, 11, 17, 19, 21 wikimedia

CONTENTS

CHAPTER ONE

CLOSE ENCOUNTER

Betty and Barney Hill

In 1961, Betty and Barney Hill saw a bright light. They pulled off a New Hampshire highway to look. Betty thought it might be a shooting star. Barney guessed a jet airplane.

Barney drove into the mountains. A pancake-shaped aircraft flew next to the car. Barney stopped. The object stopped. Barney was scared. But he walked toward the aircraft. Human-shaped figures stood behind a double row of windows.

A voice in Barney's head told him to wait. Instead, he dashed to the car. The Hills roared away. But soon Barney followed an urge to pull off the road. The Hills felt tingly and sleepy.

CHAPTER ONE

The couple woke up 35 miles away. Two hours had passed. Neither remembered what happened during the **missing time**.

Betty told her sister about the incident. But bad dreams troubled her. Barney felt anxious for no reason.

A doctor named Benjamin Simon treated the Hills with **hypnosis**. At the time, some doctors thought hypnosis helped patients get at painful memories.

Both of the Hills described being lifted into a spaceship. Strange beings did medical experiments on them. Some parts of the Hills' stories matched. Other parts differed.

Simon doubted the Hills met aliens. But Betty and Barney believed in their **close encounter**. An author wrote a book about the Hills called *The Interrupted Journey*. The Hills' experience became a television movie.

Some people took the story seriously. They believe that what happened to the Hills proved that alien beings visited Earth.

A drawing of the aircraft described by the Hills

FAST FACT

For many years, people held a special meeting in Rhode Island to tell their abduction stories.

CHAPTER TWO

THE HISTORY OF ABDUCTIONS

Scientists and engineers use weather balloons for many kinds of tests

Reports of strange aircraft began in the late 1940s. Newspapers used the term "flying saucers."

Air Force officer Edward J. Ruppelt investigated. He called these aircraft *unidentified flying objects*, or UFOs.

Some UFOs turned out to be weather balloons. Others were secret military tests. The government released information on UFOs in 2023. Many sightings turned out to be birds or drones.

CHAPTER TWO

But not every UFO report had an explanation.

A famous alien **abduction** story took place in Pascagoula, Mississippi. Calvin Parker and Charles Hickson went fishing. They claimed legless aliens kidnapped them.

"All of us moved like we were floating through air," Hickson said. The local sheriff questioned them. But he admitted the pair seemed to tell the truth.

Aliens made the news in the late 1980s. Books like *Fire in the Sky* described abductions. Whitley Strieber wrote one of the best-known books. *Communion* detailed his close encounters. His story described alien contact to millions of readers.

Calvin Parker said aliens abducted him and his co-worker Charles Hickson

FAST FACT

At first Charles Hickson told people he had passed out when he saw the spacecraft. Forty-five years later, his book described the encounter in detail.

CHAPTER TWO

Kelly Cahill claimed aliens abducted her. She lived near Melbourne, Australia. Cahill experienced missing time. Hypnosis helped her remember. Aliens examined her body, she said. They had large red eyes.

Cahill and others told their stories on TV. The big-eyed faces of aliens became familiar to everyone, not just believers.

FAST FACT

The Air Force asked scientist J. Allen Hynek to invent a way to measure UFO sightings. Seeing a UFO in the sky is a close encounter of the first kind. Hynek called coming face-to-face with beings from a UFO a close encounter of the third kind.

CHAPTER THREE

WHAT HAPPENS

People told different abduction stories. But many of them remembered:

- Strange lights;
- Floating into a spaceship;
- Being unable to move;
- It was nighttime;
- The aliens used perfect English;
- Marks on the body;
- No memory of what happened;
- Missing time.

CHAPTER THREE

Abductees in the United States often described aliens as gray skinned. Believers nicknamed the aliens "grays." A gray was shaped like a small human. Grays had large, bald heads.

"The most striking physical feature are the eyes," one woman said on the TV show *Nova*. "They're frightening, they're black, almost liquidy." Betty Hill once gave a similar description.

Paintings by Budd Hopkins hang in art museums. Hopkins also investigated alien contact stories. "They're here for their own reasons," he once said of the aliens. "And I'm not sure what those are."

John E. Mack was a famous **psychiatrist**. Hopkins told him about alien abductions.

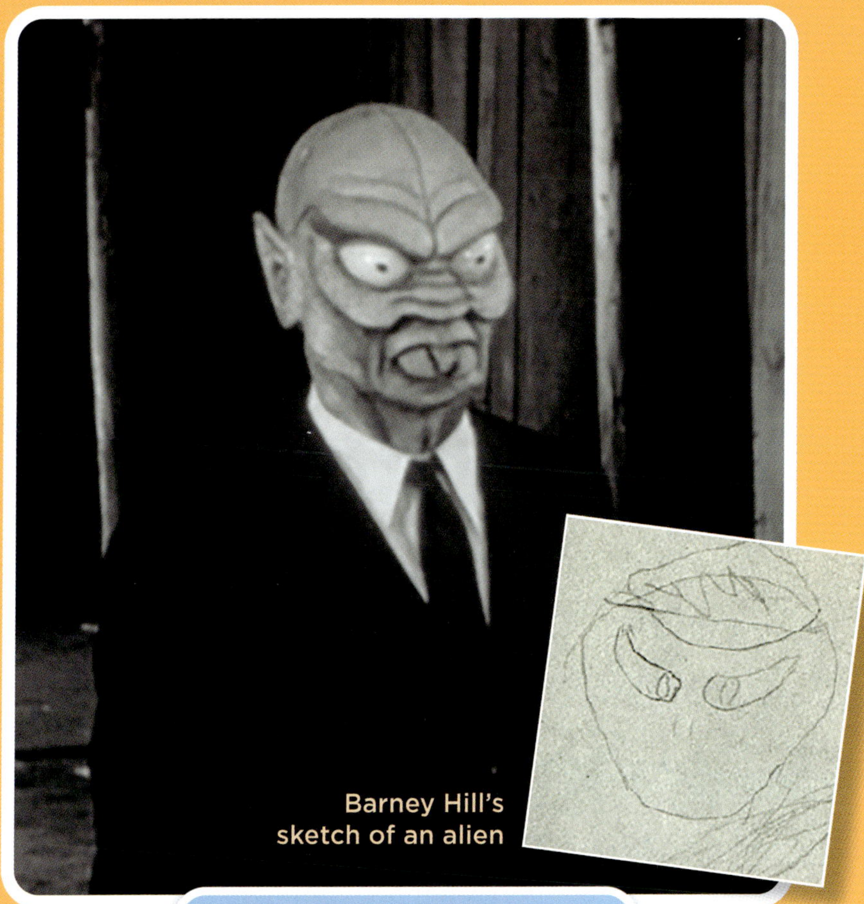
Barney Hill's sketch of an alien

FAST FACT

Aliens that looked like grays appeared on a TV show called *The Outer Limits* in 1964. One author wondered if Barney Hill had seen the episode. Maybe he imagined aliens looking that way.

CHAPTER THREE

Mack had serious doubts. But he investigated. Mack also used hypnosis. His patients remembered their abductions. Mack believed they told the truth. “If what these abductees are saying is happening to them isn’t happening,” he said, “what is?”

Hopkins and Mack thought aliens must be in contact with humans. Scientists and others began to study close encounters. They focused on facts. And the facts did not show the existence of alien abduction.

Erick von Däniken said aliens drew lines in Peru's Nazca Desert. Evidence shows that local people drew the shapes centuries ago.

FAST FACT

Erich von Däniken claimed aliens left technology on Earth in ancient times. But Von Däniken's past made him look dishonest. He went to jail after stealing money at work.

CHAPTER FOUR

SCIENCE SPEAKS UP

Carl Sagan was an **astronomer**. Sagan talked about how scientists find facts. He said, "Extraordinary claims require extraordinary **evidence**." The word *extraordinary* means very unusual.

Aliens landing on earth would be extraordinary. Showing it happens requires strong evidence. A person telling a story about a close encounter is not enough. Scientists need evidence.

The US Defense Department studied reports of aliens visiting Earth. The researchers said they had found no evidence.

Today's technology makes abduction stories hard to believe.

CHAPTER FOUR

For example, millions of people carry smartphones. A **skeptic** may ask: why has no one snapped an image of aliens? Our cameras photograph surprising events all the time. Dashcams in Russia captured a meteor strike in 2013.

Experts doubt abduction stories. But many people ignore the facts.

Believers say memories provide evidence of abductions. People remember tiny details under hypnosis. But researcher Elizabeth Loftus showed that hypnosis can create false memories.

Many abductees claim they could not move. But a 1999 study offered an explanation. Sleep **paralysis** leaves people unable to move. Sleepers around the world report similar experiences. In Japan, it's called kanashibari. One sufferer said he felt like he was lifted above the bed.

Skeptics know many people believe their own stories of alien contact. Other "abductees," though, make up the details.

FAST FACT

Why have we never found intelligent aliens in space? Peter Ward and Donald Brownlee once explained that conditions that allow human life must be very rare. In 1973, John Allen Ball stated aliens may hide themselves from us.

CHAPTER FIVE

ALIEN HOAXES

Logger Travis Walton disappeared for five days. He blamed the missing time on an abduction. Walton said he knew nothing about UFOs. But an investigator found out Walton believed in UFOs. He often discussed how he wanted to fly on one.

Even believers in alien abduction called the story a **hoax**.

People make up close encounters for many reasons. The investigator thought Walton probably used his story to escape a bad work situation.

CHAPTER FIVE

Millions looked at a 2011 YouTube video of a dead alien. Two Russian pranksters admitted they made the alien out of breadcrumbs. They meant no harm. It was a joke.

Mexican reporter Jaime Maussan believed in aliens. Maussan shocked people with a stunt. He took two tiny bodies to a government meeting. Maussan said the bodies belonged to aliens. Tests showed the bodies may have been mummies from Peru. People made fun of Maussan. But viral videos of him gained worldwide attention.

The biggest alien hoax took place in 1995. Ray Santilli claimed he owned a film of a dead alien. TV producers created a show. *Alien Autopsy* drew huge numbers of viewers.

Skeptics proved the alien was a fake. Workers on the show admitted *Alien Autopsy* was a hoax. Santilli agreed. But he insisted that a real film existed. It was just too damaged to show on TV.

No one has found evidence that aliens visit Earth. But it's likely some people will keep believing it happens.

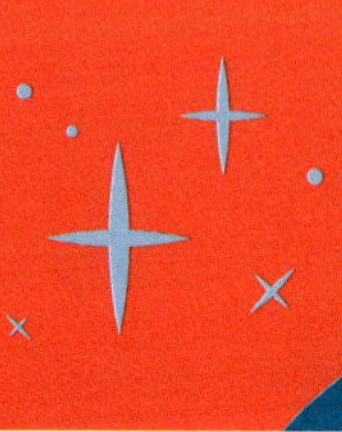

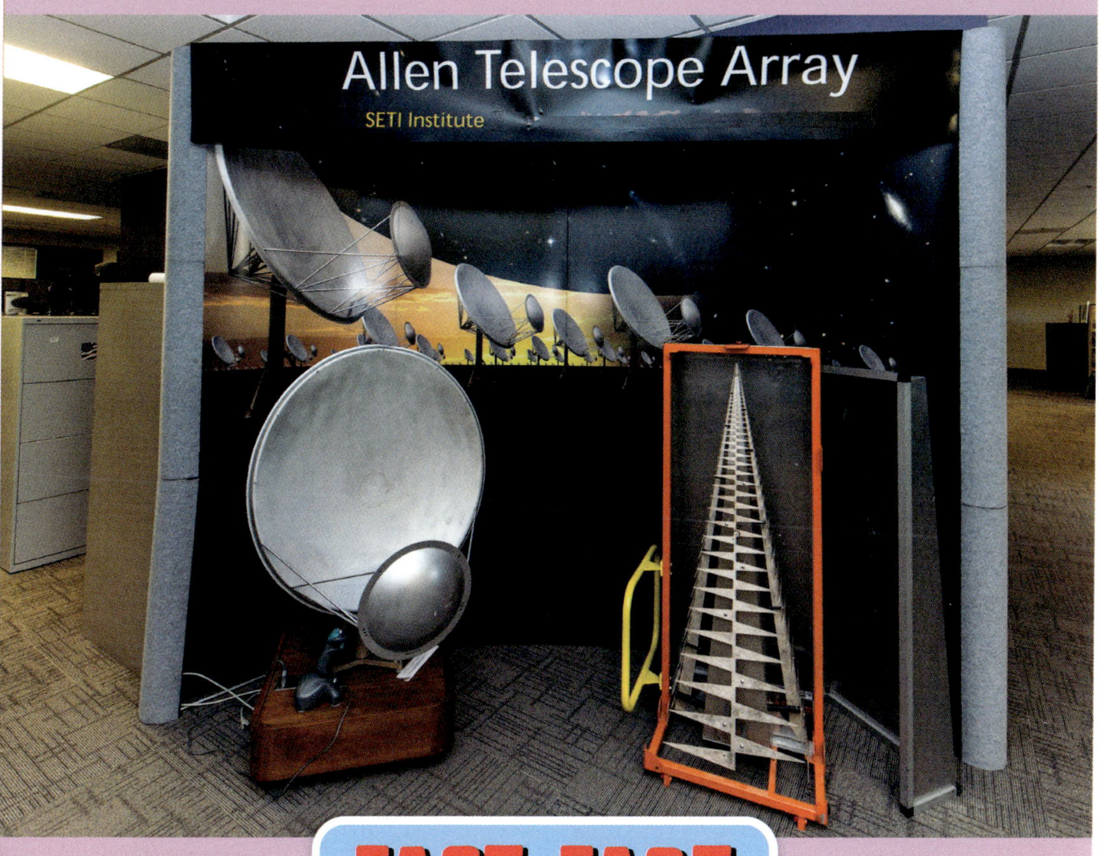

FAST FACT

The SETI Institute uses radio telescopes and other tools to search for alien life in space. Over 100 scientists and researchers work for the organization. The Institute had yet to find evidence of alien life through the year 2025.

TIMELINE

1934 Carl Sagan is born in Brooklyn, New York

1947 W. W. "Mac" Brazel finds wreckage of an unknown aircraft near Roswell, New Mexico

1957 Brazilian farmer Antônio Vilas-Boas claims aliens abducted him

1961 Betty and Barney Hill say their abduction took place in New Hampshire

1972 J. Allen Hynek invents a way to measure encounters with UFOs

1984 Thomas Pierson and Jill Tarter start the SETI Institute to search for extraterrestrial life

1993 Kelly Cahill reveals aliens abducted her in Australia

1994 John E. Mack publishes his book *Abduction*

2019 A historical society marks the site of the 1973 Pascagoula close encounter

GLOSSARY

abduction (ab-DEKH-shen)
Taking away someone by force

astronomer (AH-strahn-e-mer)
A scientist who studies stars, planets, and other bodies in space

close encounter (KLOS en-KOUNT-er)
Direct contact with aliens or a UFO

evidence (EH-ve-dens)
Facts or information that indicate something is true

hoax (HOKS)
A fake or trick used to deceive others

hypnosis (HIP-no-ses)
A trancelike state

missing time (MISS-ing TYM)
A period of time that a person cannot remember

paralysis (PA-ra-lee-sis)
The loss of the ability to move a part or all of the body

psychiatrist (se-KY-eh-trist)
A physician who treats problems of the mind

skeptic (SKEP-tik)
A person who doubts or questions an idea

FACT CHECK

1. **Which treatment helps many people remember the details of their abduction?**

   A. Watching special videos
   B. Being put under hypnosis
   C. Returning to where they saw a UFO
   D. Listening to spooky "alien music"

2. **Many people describe their abduction using which detail?**

   A. They experienced missing time
   B. The incident happened at night
   C. Aliens floated them into a spaceship
   D. All of the above

3. **Betty and Barney Hill claimed to be abducted by aliens while doing what?**

   A. Driving home on the highway
   B. Hiking in the wilderness
   C. Sleeping in their bedroom
   D. Flying a helicopter in Texas

4. **What is a popular nickname given to aliens?**

   A. Pods
   B. Triffids
   C. Klaatus
   D. Grays

Answers: B, D, A, D

FIND OUT MORE

IN PRINT

Bowman, Chris. *The Betty and Barney Hill Alien Abduction*. Hopkins, MN: Bellwether Media, 2019.

Vale, Jenna, and Janna Silverstein. *Tracking Alien Encounters*. New York: Rosen, 2018.

Mayer, Kirsten. *What Do We Know about Alien Abduction?* New York: Penguin Workshop, 2023.

ON THE INTERNET

National Geographic. "The Alien Frenzy." Via *YouTube.com*. Undated.
www.youtube.com/watch?v=0FQVfcDck-I

Public Broadcasting Service. "Carl Sagan on Alien Abduction." *Nova Online*. February 26, 1996.
https://illinois.pbslearningmedia.org/resource/arct14.sci.nvcsagan/carl-sagan-on-alien-abduction

WTIU/Public Broadcasting System. "Alien Abduction and UFOs: Why Are Grays So Common?" *Monstrum Online*. June 16, 2022.
https://video.indianapublicmedia.org/video/alien-abduction-and-ufos-why-are-grays-so-common-d5uw7p

INDEX

About the Author

Kevin Cunningham has written over 120 books on history, medicine, careers, and climate change. He lives near Chicago, Illinois. Alien contact began to interest him in grade school because UFO stories were popular at the time.